1979

Also by Michael Healey

Courageous
The Drawer Boy
Generous
The Innocent Eye Test
Kicked
The Nuttalls
Plan B
Proud
Rune Arlidge

with Kate Lynch:
The Road to Hell

1979

BY MICHAEL HEALEY

PLAYWRIGHTS CANADA PRESS
TORONTO

For professional or amateur production rights, please contact:
The Gary Goddard Agency
149 Church Street, 2nd Floor
Toronto, ON M5B 1Y4
416.928.0299, www.garygoddardagency.com/apply-for-performance-rights/

LIBRARY AND ARCHIVES CANADA CATALOGUING IN PUBLICATION
Healey, Michael, 1963-, author
        1979 / Michael Healey. -- First edition.

A play.
Issued in print and electronic formats.
ISBN 978-1-77091-750-7 (softcover).--ISBN 978-1-77091-751-4 (PDF).
--ISBN 978-1-77091-752-1 (EPUB).--ISBN 978-1-77091-753-8 (Kindle)

        1. Clark, Joe, 1939- --Drama. I. Title.

PS8565.E14A62 2017   C812'.54   C2017-900684-3
                                                  C2017-900685-1

We acknowledge the financial support of the Canada Council for the Arts, the Ontario Arts Council (OAC), the Ontario Media Development Corporation, and the Government of Canada through the Canada Book Fund for our publishing activities.

 Canada Council for the Arts   Conseil des arts du Canada ONTARIO ARTS COUNCIL
CONSEIL DES ARTS DE L'ONTARIO
an Ontario government agency
un organisme du gouvernement de l'Ontario

  Ontario
Ontario Media Development
Corporation

To the memory of Allan Lawrence, PC, QC.
A principled and generous man.

1979 premiered at the Martha Cohen Theatre, Calgary, in a production by Alberta Theatre Projects on April 6, 2017, with the following company:

Actor A: Christopher Hunt
Actor B: Jamie Konchak
Joe Clark: Philip Riccio

Director: Miles Potter
Production Dramaturg: Laurel Green
Set and Projection Design: Scott Reid
Lighting Design: David Fraser
Costume Design: Jennifer Arsenault
Sound Design: Thomas Geddes
Stage Manager: Patti Neice

The Great Canadian Theatre Company, in co-production with the Shaw Festival, presented the play in Ottawa on April 13, 2017, with the following company:

Actor A: Kelly Wong
Actor B: Marion Day
Joe Clark: Sanjay Talwar

Director: Eric Coates
Set and Lighting Design: Steve Lucas
Costume Design: Jennifer Goodman
Sound Design: Keith Thomas
Stage Manager: Allan Teichman

The production then transferred to the Shaw Festival, opening in the Jackie Maxwell Studio Theatre, Niagara-on-the-Lake, on October 1, 2017.

NOTES

The play can be staged with as few as three actors.

If three actors are used, one plays Joe Clark throughout. The other actors alternate entrances, and the distribution breaks down like this:

Actor A	Actor B
Crosbie	Lawrence
Crosbie	MacDonald
Trudeau	McTeer
MacDonald	Mulroney
Crosbie	Harper
MacDonald	Harper
Byrne	

CHARACTERS

Prime Minister Joe Clark
John Crosbie
Allan Lawrence
Flora MacDonald
Pierre Elliott Trudeau
Maureen McTeer
Brian Mulroney
Stephen Harper
Jenni Byrne

SETTING

The setting is the prime minister's office in the Centre Block of Parliament Hill. It's December 1979. There's a door upstage centre, a desk, a chair or two, a credenza. Another door leads off left, behind the desk. Wood panelling if the design is that extensive; if so, it should seem oppressively woody—wooden shutters on windows, wood cabinetry: wood wood wood.

SCENE ONE

Music off the top: "Tenth Avenue Freeze-Out," by Bruce Springsteen. The live version from the Hammersmith Odeon concert in 1975.

Projection:

> *Joe Clark was elected Canada's 16th prime minister on June 4, 1979. His was the first Progressive Conservative government in 16 years.*

Projection:

> *The Right Honourable Joe Clark.*

Prime Minister Joe CLARK *enters through the upstage door. He wears a three-piece corduroy suit that is resolutely, emphatically, brown.*

Projection:

> *Joe Clark was just 39 years old when he was elected Prime Minister.*

He seems calm. He's under some stress, and the veneer of calm is maintained through an enormous act of will. The following action is as close to an expression of anxiety as we will see for some time:

He removes his suit jacket, balls it up, and rubs his face with it, vigorously. He throws the suit jacket in a corner.

Projection:

His government, when elected, was 6 seats shy of a majority.

After a moment, he looks at the suit jacket with regret, retrieves it, and puts it on.

The sleeves are too short for his arms, as if adolescence isn't quite done with him. His long fingers taper and flatten until they are practically two-dimensional by the tips. Even when he gestures emphatically, the energy fails to flow to the ends of his hands and the effect is this: he often looks like he's holding an invisible Coke can when he's making a point. His laugh—Uh Uh Uh!—is unique and immediately identifiable. It's the only part of CLARK's *persona the actor playing him should try to emulate. As a laugh, it describes wariness, not fun.*

CLARK *sits at the desk. The music continues.*

Projection:

Wednesday, December 12, 1979.

John CROSBIE *enters. It's impossible to hear the following conversation because of the music.*

Projection:

John Crosbie, Minster of Finance.

CROSBIE: Joe.

CLARK: John.

CROSBIE: I was just about to go home, and I walked past the Liberal Christmas party—

CLARK: Right.

CROSBIE: Fucking greasy John Turner slides out, drunk as fuck, and as I'm wishing him a merry Christmas he's pointing at me and laughing.

CLARK: Right.

CROSBIE: And also sneezing. He's fucking getting wet all over me, and laughing, and I come this close to hauling off and I don't know what. I told him what I thought of that shit he pulled in committee, you know, getting all of our witnesses held over to next year even though they'd all come from all over hell's half acre to get here, and he's just standing there, staring at me wetly. But so, then, Eugene Whelan comes out, takes one look at me, one look at Turner, then gets a panicked look all over his face and drags Turner back in. I swear to God, I think something's up.

CLARK: John—

Projection:

> *The day before, December 11th, the Conservatives had finally introduced their first budget. They had been in power for more than 6 months before doing so.*

CROSBIE: You don't think they'd be stupid enough to—I mean, I'm telling ya— It's that fucking gas tax; they all fucking hate it so much, and people are gonna hate it too, which I told you—

CLARK: Okay, John—

CROSBIE: I mean, Christ! I know the plan is to govern like we won a majority, I agree with that strategy, but what if we have to fight an election in a year's time?

Projection:

> *It was a controversial document. In spite of the government's minority status, it included several harsh and divisive measures. "Short term pain for long term gain" is how Crosbie described the budget when presenting it to the House.*

And what's this I hear about you not doing any fucking polling? Is it true—Sinc Stevens tells me this goddamn government can't even get its shit together to put a simple goddamn fucking poll in the field?

CLARK: What?

CROSBIE: Eh?

CLARK: I didn't quite—

CROSBIE: WHAT?

CLARK: Did you say something about Sinc Stev—

CROSBIE notices the music for the first time.

CROSBIE: What the fuck—

CROSBIE strides around the room, looking for the source of the music. He discovers a stereo system behind a wood panel. He stabs buttons until the music stops.

CLARK: Hey. I was listening to that.

CROSBIE: And then, Trudeau walks out. They gave him a fucking chainsaw as a Christmas fucking gift. Little pecker starts waving it at me.

CLARK starts rummaging through the desk drawers.

I'm telling you, the Liberals are having too much fun for a party that says it hates being the official opposition. Joe. Joe!

He keeps looking through his drawers.

CLARK: Yes, John?

CROSBIE: Is any of this getting through?

CLARK: I've got to be honest, I missed most of it. But I get the gist.

CROSBIE: You do.

CLARK: Sure.

CROSBIE: And?

CLARK: And what, John?

CROSBIE: And what the fuck are we going to do?

A pause while CLARK rummages.

You know what I think? I think they're getting set to defeat the bud—

CLARK has found a remote and hits a button, restoring the music. The following is inaudible.

CLARK: I know. I think you may be right. Look at this.

CROSBIE: Eh?

CLARK motions him over.

CLARK: *(handing CROSBIE a paper)* This is the NDP subamendment to the Liberal confidence motion.

CROSBIE reads. He gets pink.

CROSBIE: Those fuckers. I don't get it. Those FUCKERS.

CLARK sits. CROSBIE paces.

They can't force an election. Trudeau's quit. They've no leader. How in the hell do they expect to conduct a campaign?

CLARK: This isn't conclusive.

CROSBIE: This isn't what?

CLARK: It's not proof. It could mean anything. The NDP might expect the Liberals to—

CROSBIE: Can you TURN THAT FUCKING SHIT OFF??

CLARK regards CROSBIE. He turns off the music.

CLARK: This isn't conclusive.

CROSBIE: How much evidence do you need? They're gonna vote down my budget tomorrow.

CLARK: Our budget.

CROSBIE: Right. Our budget. Our budget that I spent months kicking into existence, that has my face on it, and which I will wear like a stinking dead turbot around my neck when I go out and try to win my seat back in the next friggin' election, which will apparently be taking place not next year, but next friggin' month.

CLARK: Trudeau has resigned as leader. The NDP is broke. No one wants an election.

CROSBIE: They don't give a shit. The Liberals will fight an election with a bag of chicken shit as leader rather than sit around in opposition.

CLARK: Plus, we have the moral right to govern. We've earned that.

CROSBIE: We have the—I beg your pardon? I beg your pardon, Joe?

CLARK: We have a year to eighteen months. That's just tradition. We're only six seats shy of a majority; we've earned the right to govern. We've earned our shot is what I'm saying.

CROSBIE: We've earned our shot.

CLARK: That's what I'm saying.

CROSBIE: Is that what your polling is saying, Joe?

A pause.

When was your—sorry, *our*—last poll, Joe? When did *we* last put one in the field?

A pause.

Sinc Stevens says we haven't done any polling since August. Is that right? Joe? Huh? And let's assume for a minute the Liberals have done some polling of their own, more recently than five . . .

The incredible nature of this fact stalls him a moment.

Five. Motherfucking months ago. What do you think their polling is telling them? Do you think their polls are saying that Joe Clark has earned the *moral right* to govern for a period of between twelve and eighteen months?

CLARK: We've been busy. Tel Aviv, the energy negotiations—

CROSBIE: You've been *busy*?

CLARK: Mortgage deductibility took forever to figure out.

CROSBIE: Mort— Don't you DARE—you think I'm unaware of the problems that surrounded mortgage deductibility? The dumbest goddamn election promise ever made in the history of friggin' democratic politics, and I spilt blood to figure out a way to make motherfucking mortgage deductibility work.

CLARK: John.

CROSBIE: Yes?

CLARK: The language. Would you mind?

A pause. CROSBIE *regards* CLARK *carefully.*

CROSBIE: No, Joe. Sorry. Sorry about my use of strong language, you incredible CU—

CLARK cuts him off by turning the music back on.

CROSBIE fumes, then exits.

CLARK turns the music off. He sits.

Projection:

> *Joe Clark won leadership of the Progressive Conservatives in 1976. He defeated Brian Mulroney. He was very young. He was everyone's second choice.*

Allan LAWRENCE appears at the door. He's low-key, friendly.

Projection:

> *Allan Lawrence, Minister of Consumer and Corporate Affairs, Solicitor General.*

LAWRENCE: Joe?

CLARK: Come in, Allan.

LAWRENCE: You're hearing what's going on?

CLARK: Yeah.

LAWRENCE: What do you think?

CLARK: What do I think. I think the Liberals will let the budget pass.

LAWRENCE: You do.

CLARK: Sure. They'll hold back a few members.

LAWRENCE: Ah. Good.

A pause.

But, boy, if they don't, that'd be a . . .

CLARK: Sure would.

LAWRENCE: I mean, if they got the NDP to go along with them, then we'd be . . .

CLARK: Sure.

They blow out their cheeks at the same moment.

Projection:

Liberals 112 seats + NDP 27 seats = 139 seats.

Progressive Conservatives: 136 seats.

LAWRENCE: I mean, maybe they don't have the NDP.

CLARK: I think they could get them on board if they wanted to. Here.

CLARK hands LAWRENCE the paper he showed CROSBIE.

LAWRENCE: But you think they don't want to.

CLARK: I don't know. Maybe. I don't know.

A beat.

Depends on Les Créditistes, I guess. If they side with us.

Projection:

> *Social Credit had 5 seats in the House. PC 136 seats + 5*
> *Créditiste seats = 141 seats.*

LAWRENCE: That's why I'm here. I was just summoned to Fabien Roy's office. He says Social Credit will vote with us, but they have a condition.

CLARK: I bet they do.

Projection:

> *Several months earlier, Clark had rejected the idea of a PC–*
> *Créditiste coalition government. Créditiste leader Fabien Roy*
> *was insulted.*

LAWRENCE: They want a portion of the new gas tax revenue allocated to Quebec.

CLARK: It's federal revenue. Some of it will be allocated to Quebec.

LAWRENCE: That's what I said. He said they want it shown to be allocated to Quebec.

CLARK: Shown to be.

LAWRENCE: Shown to be.

CLARK: Shown to be how?

LAWRENCE: Fabien did not have a specific plan in that regard. I think he hopes you'll come up with something.

CLARK: Allan, is that the stupidest thing you've heard all day?

LAWRENCE: Well. The day's not over yet.

A pause.

You shouldn't do it, Joe.

CLARK: Hmm? Oh. No, I wasn't considering it. I can't start caving in to a particular province. They'll all come running. Bad enough I've got Peter Lougheed riding me like I'm a pony and it's the last day of the Ex.

Projection:

> *Peter Lougheed, Premier of Alberta, was demanding an enormous percentage of the proposed 18-cents-a-gallon gas tax.*

LAWRENCE: The—I'm sorry?

CLARK: No, sorry, I was just saying; I was saying I was a rental pony and it's the last day of the Exhibition.

LAWRENCE: Oh! The Ex. Got it. You're Peter Lougheed's pony. And he won't get off?

CLARK: Yeah. Except when Bill Davis wants a turn.

Projection:

> *Bill Davis, Premier of Ontario, hated the gas tax. Everybody hated the gas tax. Clark was committed to moving the country toward the global oil price.*

LAWRENCE: Some friends.

CLARK: Yeah. Those are some friends we got.

A beat.

LAWRENCE: Speaking of friends, Paul Yewchuk and Stan Korchinski told me they might stay away if there was a tight vote on the budget.

CLARK: Really.

LAWRENCE: They're both still pretty PO'd about not getting cabinet portfolios.

CLARK: But they're still Progressive Conservatives.

LAWRENCE: Oh yeah. Pissed enough they'd try to blackmail you, not pissed enough they'd actually quit being members of the governing party.

CLARK: Some friends.

LAWRENCE: Yeah. Plus we've got Alvin Hamilton in the hospital, Lloyd Crouse is in like Tahiti . . . By my count, we're down, uh . . .

CLARK: Like six? Six Conservative MPs travelling or sick or just being assholes?

Projection:

> *136 PC seats − 6 PCs who are ill, absent,*
> *or assholes = 130 seats.*

LAWRENCE: Yup. So, even if you did get Fabien and the Socreds on side, we might not have enough votes.

Projection:

$$+ 5 \; \text{Créditistes} = 135.$$

$$\text{Liberal} + NDP = 139 \; \text{seats.}$$

A pause.

CLARK: So how are you?

LAWRENCE: I'm good.

CLARK: Moira, the kids?

LAWRENCE: Good, good.

CLARK: Excellent. Send them my best.

LAWRENCE: Will do. I actually just spoke to Moira. She's ready to fire up the team if there's a campaign to be fought in the next little while.

CLARK: No kidding.

LAWRENCE: I think she relishes the idea of knocking on doors in the dead of winter. She believes we deserve a majority government.

A brief pause.

CLARK: Well, don't say anything to her just yet. It probably won't come to that.

LAWRENCE: Good. Okay.

LAWRENCE rises. At the door:

So, how are you? You okay?

CLARK opens his mouth to answer, but nothing comes out. He closes it again. He tries again. Is he going to cry? LAWRENCE, monumentally embarrassed, looks at his shoes and the ceiling. CLARK composes himself.

CLARK: I'm good.

LAWRENCE: Okay, see ya, Joe.

LAWRENCE departs as quickly as possible. CROSBIE appears at the door as LAWRENCE goes.

Projection:

John Crosbie.

Hey, John.

CROSBIE: Yeah whatever.

(to CLARK) Hey.

CLARK: John?

CROSBIE: You think the Liberals will hold back a few members, don't you? You think they don't want an election, don't you? That's why you're being like this.

CLARK: I don't know, John.

CROSBIE: Or do you think that even if the Liberals as a group choose to defeat the budget, there are enough of them that are too scared to run in the election? So much so that they'd defy their leadership and stay away from the vote?

CLARK: I don't know, John.

CROSBIE: Okay.

CROSBIE goes. He returns.

Projection:

> *John Crosbie.*

But are you aware we're down like five members ourselves?

CLARK: I make it six.

CROSBIE: Six! Minority government floats a tough budget, and it's got six members who can't even be bothered to show up for the friggin' vote?

CLARK: I know.

CROSBIE: Fucking hell.

CROSBIE goes. He returns.

Projection:

> *John Crosbie.*

Know what I'm gonna do?

CLARK: What's that, John.

CROSBIE: I'm gonna charter a fucking plane. And then you know what I'm gonna do?

CLARK: What, John.

CROSBIE: I'm gonna leak it that I chartered a plane. That's what I'm gonna do. Know why?

CLARK: To show everyone that we're ready to fight an election if it comes to it?

CROSBIE: To show everyone that we're ready to fight a cunting election if it comes to it. That's right!

CLARK: Okay, John.

CROSBIE: Okay!

CROSBIE goes. A beat. CLARK sits. He looks again at the NDP subamendment. Flora MACDONALD arrives at the door. She watches CLARK for a few seconds.

Projection:

Flora MacDonald, Secretary of State for External Affairs.

CLARK: *(noticing her at the door)* Hey, Flora. C'mon in.

MACDONALD: John Crosbie just ran past me like he's late to a pie eating contest.

CLARK: Yup.

MACDONALD: He's jiggling like a boiled plum.

CLARK: Yup.

She sits

MACDONALD: You've heard, I assume?

CLARK: I've heard.

MACDONALD: Think it's serious?

CLARK: Possibly. This is the NDP subamendment.

CLARK shows her the paper. She reads. Hands it back.

MACDONALD: Incredible. Broadbent. Wow.

CLARK: Wow indeed.

Projection:

> **Ed Broadbent was leader of the NDP. He decided to support the Liberals in bringing down the government.**

MACDONALD: He obviously doesn't care his party's still broke from the last election.

CLARK: Fiscal responsibility never was the NDP's strong suit.

MACDONALD: So, are you considering delaying the vote? No, don't answer that. You won't. It'd be . . . undemocratic.

CLARK: Yes.

MACDONALD: Only Joe Clark would put his political life at risk instead of simply delaying a vote.

CLARK: Not only me.

MACDONALD: Are you kidding? Do you remember how hard it was to get here? Three years of planning; three years of enormous discipline; three years of—

CLARK: No, I know. The hardest three years of our lives.

MACDONALD: Right. Not to mention the people you had to bully, or disappoint, or simply cut loose. And now we're here. And you'll risk all that because you need to know, what, that you're still good enough? That you're tough or something?

CLARK: Listen. Either I have the moral right to govern, or I don't.

MACDONALD: Jesus. That's fine in front of me, but don't let anyone else hear you talk like that.

He rises to shut the office door.

CLARK: You're probably right.

MACDONALD: I don't know if you're aware, but parliamentary politics is—

CLARK: —whatever you can get away with. Yes, I know the quote. Where are we on . . . The thing?

MACDONALD: The thing?

CLARK: Yes. You know.

MACDONALD: Yes I do. We should probably come up with a name for this operation, don't you think? Something better than "the thing."

CLARK: I'm comfortable with "the thing." It seems appropriate to the level of idiocy of the enterprise. Did you ask about the agronomists?

MACDONALD: I did. The CIA wants to stick with the movie idea.

CLARK: The movie idea makes no sense.

MACDONALD: I know.

CLARK: It makes no sense.

MACDONALD: I know.

Projection:

> *In November 1979, 6 American employees at the US consulate in Tehran escaped out a back gate as Iranians were coming in through the front. They ended up being hidden by the Canadian ambassador and his staff.*

CLARK: Canadian film scouts, looking for Middle Eastern locations. For an American film.

MACDONALD: I know, I know.

Projection:

> *Canada and the CIA were working on their exfiltration, using Canadian passports and personas for the 6 Americans.*

CLARK: Or petroleum engineers. What about saying that? We have oil; they have oil. They can be Canadian petroleum engineers. It's a more credible story.

MACDONALD: They seem pretty committed to the movie idea. I believe they even have a script.

CLARK: For the fake movie?

MACDONALD: Yes.

CLARK: Good God. They're all going to get killed, and we're going to have to wear it. When are they going to try to get out?

MACDONALD: We've created all the fake supporting documents and identities, which we sent to Iran in a diplomatic pouch. All that's left are the Iranian visa stamps on the fake Canadian passports. The CIA insisted on forging those stamps themselves. When the passports come back to us with the forged stamps, we'll send them along. We expect them any day.

CLARK: Okay.

MACDONALD: Meanwhile, there are two CIA operatives in Tehran now who are drilling the six on their new Canadian identities, preparing them for interrogations should they occur. The operatives are also experts, I'm told, in makeup and disguises.

CLARK: Makeup?

MACDONALD: And disguises.

CLARK: They're all going to get killed.

MACDONALD: Thought you'd appreciate that detail.

CLARK: Okay. Anything else?

MACDONALD: No. I'll let you know when the passports are returned to us.

CLARK: Thanks.

She rises

MACDONALD: You know, Joe. It wouldn't be considered weakness to make a few moves to hold onto power.

CLARK: I'm not worried about looking weak.

MACDONALD: You sure?

CLARK: I've looked weak my whole career. Look how far it's gotten me.

MACDONALD: True enough.

CLARK: Hey. How's it going. We haven't checked in for a while.

MACDONALD: Fine. No complaints. Learning the file.

CLARK: You're doing great. But how's it going?

MACDONALD: Joe. You can't take care of me. I can't come to you whenever someone calls me "baby" or puts a hand on my behind.

CLARK: No, I know. I'm just saying—

MACDONALD: You ever ask Erik Nielsen if he gets groped?

CLARK: He's old and wrinkly. Groping Erik would require you to genuflect or something.

MACDONALD: Sorry?

CLARK: He—I'm saying you'd have to bend way down to fondle his bottom.

MACDONALD: Ah.

CLARK: Due to his age.

CLARK's phone rings.

MACDONALD: Okay. See you, Joe.

CLARK: Yeah. Hey, Flora, stick around, why don't you. There might be a budget vote later or something.

She goes. He picks up the phone.

Hello. What? Why? No, I mean *(starts to whisper)* why is he here? Okay. Okay.

He hangs up.

Jesus.

He looks around. He goes through a door that's located behind his desk.

After a beat, "Poets" by the Tragically Hip begins playing.

Projection:

Pierre.

Elliott.

Trudeau.

TRUDEAU enters, dancing to the music. He holds a very small chainsaw. After a bit of dancing, he notices the audience. He's now dancing for them.

CLARK enters, watches for a while. He then finds the remote and clicks off the music.

TRUDEAU: Joooooe.

CLARK: Pierre.

TRUDEAU: Look what they gave me.

CLARK: It's . . . That's a nice one. What is that, a Husqvarna?

TRUDEAU: *(like he's stupid)* No, Joe. It's a chainsaw.

CLARK: Right. But—

TRUDEAU: You know, for cutting down trees. Making lumber. You know.

CLARK: I—yes, I do.

TRUDEAU: Or logs for the fire. To put in the fireplace.

CLARK: I, yes.

TRUDEAU: Honestly, Joe, it's like you've never been outside.

CLARK: I was actually—

TRUDEAU: So, I don't know if you've ever been begged for anything, Joe. Have you? Really been begged for something? Because I have. People have, at various points in my life, begged me for things. And not just, you know, on the phone, "Come home now, I beg you; I don't care where you've been or with whom, just please, I beg you return home to us," not that kind of thing. I don't mean domestic begging. I mean begging in the professional sphere. People have begged me for lots of things, over the years, to lend my various talents to various activities, some righteous, some insipid. But you've never seen, Joe, *real* begging until you've witnessed a group of men and women who smell an opportunity to reacquire power, but who have come to the realization that none of them is qualified to lead and they need you to do it.

Projection:

> *Having lost the election earlier that year, Trudeau announced his resignation as Liberal leader, and his retirement from politics. He was marking time until the Liberal Party leadership convention, planned for early 1980.*

CLARK: And what did you tell them? These people?

TRUDEAU: Resolutely, I told them no.

CLARK: I see.

Projection:

> *The chainsaw was a gift from Liberal MPs who hoped he would change his mind about retirement and return as leader to "cut down the government."*

TRUDEAU: I remain firm in my resolve to disengage from public life. In favour of life itself. My boys need a father.

Projection:

> *Trudeau and his wife had separated; Trudeau had custody of their 3 boys.*

CLARK: Yes.

TRUDEAU: Also, please, Joe, this job? Prime minister? It's revolting. One is nothing more than a glorified civil servant and loudmouthed shill. Traipsing across the world trying to advance the interests of an ungrateful country, an in fact openly hostile country.

CLARK: I see.

TRUDEAU: Having done the job, I can't honestly understand why anyone would ever agree to being prime minister of Canada. It's like having rotten chum tossed at you while you shake your, ehm, pompoms and sing a show tune.

CLARK: Colourful.

TRUDEAU: You know, with a little hat in front of you to collect change.

CLARK: Busking.

TRUDEAU: Hmm? No. You know, like a street performer. With a hat to collect change on the sidew—

CLARK: Yes. Yes.

TRUDEAU: I could not be happier to be leaving politics. I came here to tell you that, Joe.

CLARK: Thank you. And thank you, Pierre, for your years of service to the country.

TRUDEAU: Hmmm. My legacy will be . . . fraught, I think. Mixed.

CLARK: No no. You've done an enormous amount for the country.

Projection:

> *Reforms to the public service had created chaos and widespread unhappiness among bureaucrats.*
>
> *Inflation was 9.8%.*
>
> *Unemployment was 8.4%.*
>
> *The October Crisis of 1970 had damaged Trudeau's reputation as a civil libertarian.*
>
> *Wage and price controls were having a high social cost with little economic benefit.*
>
> *Official bilingualism as a method of staving off Quebec separatism was unpopular everywhere else in the country.*
>
> *Trudeau's refusal to negotiate power-sharing with provinces was stoking separatist sentiment in Quebec.*
>
> *His focus on Quebec left the West feeling excluded.*
>
> *His proposal to abolish the Indian Act labelled him an assimilationist.*
>
> *Federal debt had exploded since 1972, as had federal spending.*
>
> *Trudeau hated the press. The feeling was increasingly mutual.*

TRUDEAU: Well, it's been a grand experiment, at any rate. So: tell me. What are you going to do?

CLARK: Regarding?

TRUDEAU: The vote later. How will you avoid it?

CLARK: Why on earth would I tell you my strategy?

TRUDEAU: Ooooh, come on, Joe. I won't tell anyone. After all, we want the same thing. For your government to survive. Even if every other Liberal in this building is desperate to bring you down. All I want is to sail through the next few months doing as little as possible until they come up with my replacement.

Projection:

> *Trudeau had recently cancelled an appearance at a Liberal policy conference, claiming he had the flu. He was photographed in New York City that evening entering a discotheque with a model on his arm.*

So what is it? Are you going to delay the vote somehow?

CLARK: No.

TRUDEAU: No? You realize there's no way I'm going to be able to hold the caucus back? I believe they're going to pull a couple of our guys out of the hospital for the vote.

CLARK: Yes.

TRUDEAU: Broadbent won't back down. His subamendment is going to be palatable to Liberals.

CLARK: I've got a copy right here.

TRUDEAU: And my count has you losing even if the Socreds back you. Even if I abstain. Not that I could.

CLARK: I wouldn't expect you to.

TRUDEAU: Then what? Some sort of procedural play that lets you keep power after losing the vote?

CLARK: No.

TRUDEAU looks at CLARK.

TRUDEAU: Are you bluffing?

CLARK: No.

TRUDEAU: No, you're not. So you intend to . . . lose?

CLARK is silent. TRUDEAU walks around. A few beats while he thinks. Finally:

You cunt.

CLARK: Pierre?

TRUDEAU: You disrespect power. It's the only unforgivable thing in politics. Is it your age? I don't know. You're young, but you're not stupid. But you have no respect for it. It's just . . . You know, God, when I think of everything I went through, not only to acquire power, but also the million shitty things I had to do once I had it to maintain it. Every moronic hand I shook. Every piece of advice I was forced to listen to, from well-meaning idiots. Every dollar I raised, every baby I shook, every goddamned plate of awful food I ate in front of people! Speeches, carefully crafted and a joy to deliver, soured in my mouth from the sheer idiotic repetition of them! Repeated until I thought I'd go mad, until I thought going mad would be preferable to mouthing the wretched speech one more time.

CLARK: Listen, I've got things I should be—

TRUDEAU: All I went though, just so I could wield a little power. It's not a lot of power; you must realize it by now, being prime minister isn't like running a bank or owning a few newspapers or anything, it's not even like manning the door at a popular disco—a, what do you call those guys, hulking—

CLARK: The doorman?

TRUDEAU: No, not the doorman. *The* doorman. A doorman at a disco has more power at his disposal than I did. Than you do. But nonetheless, it's yours. You have it, however briefly. And the fact that you do nothing, at this stage, to protect it, to keep it, it's incredible, Joe.

CLARK: What's incredible is that you would try to take it away from me this early in my mandate.

TRUDEAU: THAT'S MY JOB. That is my job, Joe.

CLARK: If you wanted to, you could go into that Christmas party, tell your caucus the timing is wrong for bringing down this government. Let's get our own house in order first, you could say, get a leader in place, then develop a set of policies to counter the Conservatives, give the country an alternative. And *then* confront the government. Have an election on merits.

TRUDEAU: Sure, or I could stand amid a pack of rabid, retarded jackals and recite William Blake. Individually, the members of the Liberal caucus are decent, pleasant men. Many unmolested by intelligence, but happy. But, together, they are an amoral beast, hungry for nothing but the dollop of power you possess and seem perfectly content to throw their way. If you are under the impression I can save you, Joe, disabuse yourself.

CLARK: I don't need you to save me, Pierre; I thought you might be compelled to do the right thing here.

TRUDEAU: The right thing? Her Majesty's Loyal Opposition giving your fledgling government time to bloom through some sort of morbid passivity isn't the *right thing to do*. Joe. The right thing here is to keep what you've achieved by any means available to you. You may not have been listening closely when you were sworn in, but you're now obliged to fuck, eat, or kill to stay behind that desk. Fuck, eat, kill. For as long as you can. That's what you agreed to.

CLARK: I agreed to pursue a set of policies that I believe are in the country's interest.

TRUDEAU: Which you will be unable to do from your chesterfield in Calgary when you lose!

CLARK: High River.

TRUDEAU: What?

CLARK: I'm from—God. You know nothing about me. I know everything about you and you know nothing about me.

TRUDEAU: Well whose fault is that!

CLARK: Listen: Can I ask you a favour?

TRUDEAU: Oh, yes, by all means.

CLARK: I've given you regular briefings on the very delicate situation we find ourselves in in Iran.

TRUDEAU: You have.

CLARK: Confidential briefings.

TRUDEAU: Indeed.

CLARK: Fair to say I've kept you abreast of what we're facing in Iran, what the dangers are, what the stakes are?

TRUDEAU: More than fair.

CLARK: Well, given that's the case, would you mind not repeatedly bringing up the Iran situation in Parliament and accusing me of inaction? Especially since you know the opposite is true?

TRUDEAU: But, Joe—you are conducting this operation, this extraction of the Americans, in secret. And I have been made party to that secret. You can't reveal the secret. So I cudgel you in the House with the secret you can't reveal. What am I missing?

CLARK: Nothing. You're not missing anything. I'm saying, please stop doing that. Do me the courtesy. The way I've done you the courtesy of keeping you in the loop.

TRUDEAU: I will not. I will not subvert our democracy in the interest of *courtesy*. I will not abuse the sanctity of the House of Commons so I can offer you the same courtesy you chose to show me. It would be wrong.

CLARK: You stand there and lie every time you ask me a question you already know the answer to.

TRUDEAU: The leader of Her Majesty's Loyal Opposition lies in the House? Can it be so? But how have things come to this?

CLARK: You abuse the institution when you accuse me of things you know are untrue. You diminish Parliament when you do that,

Pierre; don't pretend you don't know what I'm saying. It's meant to be an honest exchange of points of view in there, on the public record. It's rough-and-tumble, and I—

TRUDEAU: Shush. Shush.

CLARK: —I understand that; I know that we are suppo—

TRUDEAU: SHUSH, JOE. Please.

CLARK is silent. TRUDEAU is thinking. A substantial pause.

Oh God. Oh no.

CLARK: What.

TRUDEAU: Ooooooh no.

CLARK: Pierre?

TRUDEAU: Everyone around me mocks you. You know that.

CLARK: I, yes, I assumed as much.

TRUDEAU: I never did.

CLARK: I appreciate that.

TRUDEAU: But now I realize something: by resisting the urge to mock you, by shutting down those that did, I made the mistake of overestimating you.

CLARK: Um.

TRUDEAU: There's actually less to you than meets the eye.

CLARK: Um.

TRUDEAU: Remember when I lost the election?

CLARK: When, yes, I won it.

TRUDEAU: Remember when Lévesque said that now Quebec could have a referendum on sovereignty, because I was no longer in power?

CLARK: Yes. He's moving forward rather quickly. We're monitoring the—

TRUDEAU: I thought he just meant he knew he could never make the case for Quebec's exclusion from Canada while a Quebecker was prime minister. But that's not what he meant.

CLARK: It's not?

TRUDEAU: No, not just that. He also meant he wants you. He needs you.

CLARK: You mean he—

TRUDEAU: This is horrible. Now I'm gonna have to . . . Aw Christ on a Popsicle stick.

CLARK: Um.

TRUDEAU: He wants you leading the No side. He knows he can win a referendum if he's fighting you. He knows he can't win if he's fighting me.

CLARK: That seems—

TRUDEAU: He knows you'll take a decent, reasoned approach to the fight. He knows he can beat you because your ethics are two-dimensional. What's your whole approach to Quebec? A community of communities?

CLARK: The country, yes, is a community of communities, and Quebec is def—

TRUDEAU: Meaningless. What you just said is absolutely devoid of meaning. But you know what? It's enough for Lévesque to flay you with. You'll start there, with your meaningless platitude, then when that doesn't work you'll make, what, economic arguments? Quebec will suffer financially if it secedes?

CLARK: But it's true—

TRUDEAU: Then when you become desperate, you'll appeal to sentiment. And finally, at the end, with the destruction of the country mere days away, you'll resort to begging.

CLARK: It won't come to that.

TRUDEAU: Yes it fucking will! And then, a week before the referendum, with Lévesque in the lead, you'll stand in front of your cabinet and weep because you'll realize you'll be held responsible for Quebec's departure. He'll destroy you, and then destroy the country. With Quebec gone, how long before Alberta secedes? Then that'll be it! The whole experiment, Canada, started by a Conservative drunk and finished off by a Conservative nobody!

CLARK: I'm a Progressive Conservative nobody.

TRUDEAU: You can't stop him. Nobody can. Except me. Oh God. For the love of Mary, I can't frigging quit!

TRUDEAU goes quiet. His mood darkens.

CLARK: Listen, Pierre. I can handle the Quebec thing. I can handle Lévesque. I'm going to call a first ministers' conference in the new year, head him off. A bit of arm twisting, a bit of persuasion, a bit of bribery and he'll—

TRUDEAU: This is disgusting. I curse my conscience. I curse it. I have to come back.

CLARK: No, no you don't; now, Pierre—

TRUDEAU: I do. I have to return to politics; I have to win the next election; I have to lead the No side. I have to defeat Lévesque; I have to save the country. I have to do it all.

Projection:

> *Trudeau announced he was returning to lead the Liberal Party*
> *in a press conference on December 18th.*

My poor boys.

TRUDEAU turns to go.

CLARK: Pierre.

TRUDEAU stops.

Your chainsaw.

TRUDEAU: You keep it, Joe. You'll get to use it sooner than I.

TRUDEAU trudges away, despondent.

A beat. He returns.

On second thought, you'd better let me have it, Joe. You'll only hurt yourself.

CLARK *hands* TRUDEAU *the chainsaw. As he does:*

CLARK: I just beat you, a few months ago. What makes you so certain I won't do it again?

TRUDEAU: Is that the way you see it? That you beat me in this last election?

Projection:

Results of the last election:

PC 136.

Liberal 114.

NDP 26.

Social Credit 6.

CLARK: Of course.

TRUDEAU: Joe. They didn't elect you. They rejected me. They wanted to teach me a lesson.

CLARK: Well, but, if that's true, what makes you think they won't want to teach you the same lesson this time around?

TRUDEAU: I might as well tell you. It hardly makes a difference. This time I just won't say anything. Not a thing. I'll do it on charm.

TRUDEAU, *immensely sad, goes.*

CLARK: Who will rid me of this turbulent priest? As they say.

Projection:

> *In the 1980 campaign, Trudeau kept appearances and speeches brief. When he spoke, he spoke only of Clark's weaknesses. He scheduled no press conferences. Zero. When the press petitioned him to hold one, he responded in Latin.*
>
> *Trudeau refused to participate in a leaders' debate.*
>
> *The single most significant act of Trudeau's campaign: going to Harry Rosen and buying several new suits in the latest style.*
>
> *1980 election results:*
>
> *Liberal 147.*
>
> *PC 103.*
>
> *NDP 32.*
>
> *Social Credit 0.*
>
> *But what the hell. You didn't come to the theatre to read stuff.*

CLARK is seated. A woman appears at the door. She's vibrating with some kind of energy.

Projection:

> *Maureen McTeer. Clark's wife.*

CLARK: Maureen.

MCTEER: Joe.

CLARK: How'd it go? How'd you do?

MCTEER: I did well.

CLARK: Which one was it?

MCTEER: Real estate.

Projection:

> *Maureen McTeer that day wrote the 8th of 14 bar exams.*
> *She was 27 years old.*

CLARK: Uh huh. And how are you, you know, feeling?

She kicks the door closed without taking her eyes off him.

MCTEER: I think you know how I'm feeling.

A beat between them. She advances slowly. He looks for the remote, pushes a button. "Love TKO" by Teddy Pendergrass plays. MCTEER stops, makes a face. She goes to the sound system, pushes stop, then pushes another button. "Heavy Chevy" by Alabama Shakes comes on. She turns up the volume, turns to CLARK. She advances on him, and, as the lights fade, CLARK shoves everything off his desk.

Blackout.

SCENE TWO

The lights rise and the music fades. CLARK *is tugging his brown clothes back on.* MCTEER *tucks a single strand of hair behind her ear.*

MCTEER: You know who else was there writing the exam? The young NDP guy. Bob Rae.

CLARK: Really? He's been busy.

CLARK *finds the subamendment on the floor, hands it to* MCTEER.

Here's a motion he's about to present in the House.

MCTEER: A non-confidence motion? Over what, the budget? He wouldn't dare.

CLARK: I suspect he would.

MCTEER: The Liberals won't play along. They have no leader.

CLARK: It's possible I may have just accidentally convinced Pierre to stay on as their leader.

MCTEER: What?

CLARK: Yeah. Not on purpose. Basically just by standing here.

MCTEER: Oh God. OH GOD!

CLARK: Darling?

MCTEER: There are six more exams I have to write. I can't do that during an election campaign.

CLARK: If it comes to it, I'll call the head of the Ontario Bar and ask him to give you an extension.

MCTEER: Like fuck you will.

CLARK *giggles.*

CLARK: I really, really like it a lot when you curse.

MCTEER: The NDP propped up the Liberals for two years. They won't do the same for you?

CLARK: Nope. Broadbent wants an election.

MCTEER: They should like mortgage deductibility.

CLARK: They should. They hate the gas tax more. Everybody hates the gas tax.

MCTEER: There's a refund for low-income families, right?

CLARK: A rebate, yes. It doesn't kick in for a year, though.

MCTEER: Move it up. Say you'll implement the rebate immediately.

CLARK: We need the year of revenue. The debt is huge—

MCTEER: Tell the NDP you're willing to implement the rebate immediately, and if they don't support you, you'll leak to the press that they could have done the right thing for working-class families but refused.

CLARK: No.

MCTEER: No? What do you mean n—

CLARK: I won't! I won't, Maureen.

MCTEER: Joe—

CLARK: I haven't done anything. I haven't done a single thing in this job, Maureen. It's been months, and all I've done is lose fights in public and stall things I promised and back down over things I said I believed in! And meanwhile, MEANWHILE, my own people can't disguise how little they respect me.

MCTEER: Who cares if they respect you? They have to do what you say.

CLARK: This budget was all I cared about. Getting this budget right was the only thing I wanted. We took our time. The only reason to put ourselves through the hell of getting elected is so we can put the finances of the country in order. People will suffer for generations if we don't fix what Trudeau did. People are suffering now!

MCTEER: You don't have to sell me—

CLARK: So this is it. This is the hill to die on. This budget, right now. Get this through, start down this path, and then all the bullshit, all the Joe Clark, who's he? Some asshole from out West. Sure he's got a hot wife, but really he's a nobody with no ideas that nobody has to listen to because, I mean, look at the guy, friggin' brown suit, not a fancy little Quebec dude with a convertible. He's just some guy, nobody likes him; he just backed into the job, did nothing to earn the leadership, did nothing to convince the country his ideas are worthy; he's just a shit guy from nowhere who has no business anywhere near the public trust. You know? Like: frig that guy. Frig him. Frig him and all his hard work and his devotion to the country; I mean, that part's just pathetic—oh, he wants to help people; he wants to reform the country's finances, isn't he so special—just: *frig that guy.*

A beat. Now he's dizzy. He bends over, puts his hands on his knees.

Oh boy.

MCTEER: *(going through her purse)* I've got a sandwich in here somewhere.

CLARK: Thanks.

He eats the sandwich.

MCTEER: Joe. I've never seen you like this. Listen to me: I want you to know that it is just a moment, what's happening now. You're tired and frustrated and feeling trapped. You see no options, and this thing is looming, and you're stuck. But this is just a moment. There's a moment after this one, and one after that, and after that. And because of who you are, Joe, this thing will turn around. Because you're right, because you're smart, and because you've earned the right to be here, this will all work out for you. Do you hear me, Joe?

CLARK: Is this turkey?

MCTEER: No, it's— It's tuna, Joe.

CLARK: Oh yeah.

MCTEER: Who can't tell tuna when they taste tuna?

CLARK: Sorry. I'm feeling a bit whoop-y. Thanks for the sandwich.

MCTEER: Joe, do you even want this job?

CLARK: Sure I do.

MCTEER: Why?

CLARK: At the moment, I couldn't actually tell you.

MCTEER: Let me remind you then. Because the psyche of the country is pretty delicate right now. Your countrymen are not patriots. Self-interest rules. And too many people are suffering as a consequence of the selfishness that infects us. And you have an idea about how the country might cohere. You want to give people who have no reason to hope a reason to hope. You want to give people a vision of the country they can believe in, get behind, and prosper as a result of. And listen, Joe: you're not temperamentally suited for this job. You're not a politician. We both know that. But here's the thing: people see you, they become attached to something about you. It's your decency. Your decency, Joe, has a charisma. Charisma is the only thing a politician requires, and you have a sort nobody's ever seen before. You're a decent person, and people, when they are at their best, insist on being led by decency. It's that simple. So you're here, and it's no accident. And you're doing something hard, and that's your job. You can be responsible for enormous change, Joe. You can affect the lives of so many people for the better.

CLARK: Do you have any water? This turkey's a little dry.

There's a pitcher of water on the credenza; she pours him a glass.

MCTEER: Remember when you won the leadership of the party, my darling? We thought it was a miracle at the time. We thought winning this last election was a miracle. But they weren't miracles, Joe. You made them happen. You did. And you belong here. Now: it's tough here because it has to be; the development of consensus is the only way to pursue the public good, and so—

CLARK: *(hands the water glass back)* Thank you.

MCTEER: —and so that's why you're here. And that's why you'll figure something out. If not having this vote is the thing that serves your goals, Joe, you'll figure it out. I know you will. There's a way to avoid this vote and its consequences, Joe, and I know in my heart that you'll come up with some way, some method of not having this vote.

CLARK: I mean, the way to not have the vote is to just not have it.

MCTEER: What do you mean?

CLARK: Well, the government controls the parliamentary agenda, so if we want to not have the vote, we can . . . Just not.

MCTEER: You can . . . change the agenda?

CLARK: Yeah. Just do that.

MCTEER: Okay. That . . . um, that seems simple.

CLARK: Sure.

MCTEER: Okay! Way to go! I knew you could do it!

CLARK: Sure. Except it's the wrong thing to do.

MCTEER: It's the— I'm sorry?

She looks at him carefully. A beat. He shrugs.

That's . . . um. Joe? There's something wrong with you.

CLARK: Sweetie?

MCTEER: I was given to understand there was a crisis.

CLARK: Well, I guess depending on how you look at it, this is as crisis-y as it gets.

MCTEER: But— Hmm. I actually think there's something wrong with you, Joe. I think Ottawa has made you, um, stupid. I'm sorry. I love you.

CLARK: Love you too.

MCTEER: It's *wrong*? To do something utterly within the rules that gets you what you want?

CLARK: But I mean, we're still in the same boat. The numbers don't change; we just delay the vote.

MCTEER: Giving the geniuses, the incredible brains trust you've surrounded yourself with, time to come up with a solution. Time to get people on board, Joe, develop consensus, you know? The basis of democracy? Consensus?

CLARK: I've heard of consensus, yes.

MCTEER: Or twist arms, call in favours, or blackmail people.

CLARK: The other levers of democracy.

MCTEER: Joe! Just don't have the vote if you don't have to have the vote!

CLARK: I've staked everything on this budget, and all my credibility rests on getting it passed. Right now.

MCTEER: No, I get it, it means a lot, but—

CLARK: Maureen. Maureen. It means everything. If I can't do it now, I can't do it. It can't be done. There are terms on which I can do the job, and if they get tossed out, I don't want the job.

MCTEER: I see. Okay.

A pause.

So that's it. I can't convince you to do the sensible thing?

CLARK: Not at the expense of the right thing, no.

MCTEER: And I'm on the record as trying to talk you out of this incredibly dumb thing you're bent on doing? I've tried, right, to keep you from throwing away your government, your job, everything?

CLARK: So noted, yes.

MCTEER: Joe Clark. I just fucking—

CLARK: Sweetie?

MCTEER: I love you so hard, Joe Clark. I love you so much.

CLARK: I love you too.

MCTEER: I'm so happy!

CLARK: You are?

MCTEER: You have no idea! Because I've made sure you have no idea! Oh, Joe! I hate this fucking place so much!

CLARK: You—

MCTEER: And now maybe it's over! Oh God! I loathe all of this so! The dimwittedness, the naked but pointless power mongering! The people! Oh God! And the relentless, crushing sexism of the place! If I have one more hand on my ass at a motherfucking cocktail party—do you know when the queen mother came to town a couple of months ago I was introduced to her as Mrs. Clark over and over again!

Projection:

> **McTeer kept her surname after they married; people considered**
> **this evidence of Clark's weakness.**

CLARK: Who did?

MCTEER: They all did! They all do it when you're out of earshot! Everyone calls me Mrs. Clark! Especially the wives. And they did it that day, those *women*, to humiliate me. I walked the queen mother to her car at the end of the lunch and she looked me right in the eye and called me Ms. McTeer. She pointed out that her daughter had kept her name, and if it was good enough for the queen of England, then it was probably good enough for me. I could have kissed her. But think about it, Joe: the people around here aren't as progressive as the British fucking monarchy!

CLARK: That's some BS right there.

MCTEER: This place is small-minded and hateful and if you're willing to give it all up on principle, Joe Clark, then I'm so happy I could fuck you right in half.

CLARK: Hee hee hee.

MCTEER: C'mere!

CLARK: No, I, no, darling? Darling. As much as I'd like you to . . . do that thing you said, I'm not giving up. I'm going to lose the vote, then have the election, come back with a majority, and then pass exactly the budget bill I want, with the full consent and mandate of the people.

MCTEER: You're willing to take that chance?

CLARK: What chance? They just elected us. Literally nothing has changed since they did that. And if we're smart about allocating resources in the campaign, I'm sure we can pick up the few seats we need for a majority.

MCTEER: Is that what your polling is telling you?

A beat.

CLARK: Uhhh.

MCTEER: What.

CLARK: Well, we've been busy, and, uhh . . .

MCTEER: When was your last poll?

CLARK: Well. We've been really busy, and—

MCTEER: Joe! No polling? What!

CLARK: Yeah, it's . . .

MCTEER: So, basically, Joe Clark, you're freeballing this whole thing?

CLARK: Uhh, uh huh.

MCTEER: That's it. I can't stand it anymore. Take those things off.

MCTEER advances on CLARK's pants. Flora MACDONALD appears at the door.

Projection:

Flora MacDonald.

MACDONALD: Joe— Oh, hi, Maureen.

MCTEER: Hi, Flora.

MACDONALD: You still writing the bar exams?

MCTEER: I had real estate this morning.

MACDONALD: Everybody says bar exams are staggeringly dull. How are you finding them?

MCTEER: I'm finding them almost comically aphrodisic.

MACDONALD: Super. Well, I don't want to interrupt, just wanted to say, Joe, the diplomatic pouch we've been waiting for has arrived.

CLARK: Great. Good.

MCTEER: I'd better go. Keep me posted?

CLARK: You bet.

She kisses him.

MCTEER: See you soon, Flora. Merry Christmas if we don't.

MACDONALD: Merry Christmas, Maureen.

MCTEER goes.

Do you want to see the CIA's handiwork before we send the fake passports to Iran?

CLARK: God, no. Yes. I'd better take a look.

MACDONALD: I'll send over the pouch.

CLARK: Thanks.

MACDONALD: We still on for later?

CLARK: Sorry?

MACDONALD: The vote. We still having a budget vote later?

CLARK: Far as I know, yes.

MACDONALD: You know, I've been at this a while.

Projection:

> *Flora MacDonald started as John Diefenbaker's secretary.*
> *His secretary.*

CLARK: Sure.

MACDONALD: I've seen some things.

CLARK: I bet.

MACDONALD: Never seen anything like you.

CLARK: I'm not special.

MACDONALD: Not out there you're not. But here? Around here, you're like a unicorn.

CLARK: In that I mostly don't exist.

MACDONALD: What an odd thing to say.

CLARK: I have a theory that people cling to power, focus on it to the point of hysteria, because it's a proxy for life itself. People who have had a taste of power, it feels like life, like being alive. And they become desperate to keep it because losing it is too much like death.

MACDONALD: Huh.

CLARK: But I've never been afraid of death. I don't know why. Too dumb I guess. I'm more afraid of living a wasted life.

MACDONALD: Joe Clark, philosophic unicorn death-baiter.

CLARK: You can put that under my official prime ministerial portrait.

Projection:

It was 2008 before Clark's portrait was put up in Parliament.

MACDONALD: See you around.

CLARK: See you later.

She turns to go. Brian MULRONEY *is at the door. Projection:*

Brian Mulroney.

MACDONALD: Oh! Hello, Brian. Where did you come from?

MULRONEY: I was just . . . around.

MACDONALD: Creepy.

She goes.

MULRONEY: She's great. Hey!

CLARK: Brian. How are you?

MULRONEY: Nothing. I was just in the neighbourhood.

CLARK: O . . . kay.

MULRONEY: Thought I'd say hi.

CLARK: How're things at IOC?

MULRONEY: You know, if you ever find yourself running a steel company, I recommend doing it while commodity prices are booming.

Projection:

> *After he lost the PC leadership to Clark in 1976, Mulroney became a vice president at Iron Ore Company of Canada. By 1979 he was President.*

CLARK: Uh uh uh!

MULRONEY: You'll look like a genius.

CLARK: You look hale, at any rate.

A beat.

Healthy, I mean.

MULRONEY: I quit drinking.

CLARK: Really! You!

MULRONEY: Had to do it.

CLARK: Doctor's orders?

MULRONEY: Mila's. Anyhoo, just stopping by. Just saying hi.

CLARK: Okay.

A pause.

So . . .

MULRONEY: Look. Whatever happens. I want you to know the party's behind you. Whatever happens. I've been authorized to tell you that.

CLARK: Well, thanks, Brian. I appreciate that.

MULRONEY: WHATEVER happens.

CLARK: Okay. Thanks.

MULRONEY: Including, and this I know might seem far-fetched: including the possibility you'll lose tonight's vote.

CLARK: Great. I appreciate it.

MULRONEY: How's it looking, by the way?

CLARK: It's, well, it's gonna be tight.

MULRONEY: Yeah . . .

CLARK: Yeah.

MULRONEY: That's the word around town, yeah.

CLARK: Yeah.

A pause.

MULRONEY: So, um, anyway. Have you given any thought to any . . . Actions you might take in the next little while?

CLARK: You mean, as regards the vote?

MULRONEY: No. I mean, I guess I mean, um. Well: you know the party brass has been a little confused by your approach to patronage appointments over the last few months.

CLARK: They have?

MULRONEY: Oh, yeah. This is news to you?

CLARK: No. I guess not.

MULRONEY: Joe. You haven't appointed anybody. To anything.

CLARK: I've been busy.

MULRONEY: I get it; but, Joe, you did not win that election alone. There are a lot of people who helped you, right?

CLARK: Sure.

MULRONEY: Well, some of them expect something for their help.

CLARK: As they should. I know how things work, and I'm happy to see that positions are filled with people that deserve them.

MULRONEY: Are you? Are you, Joe, because—

CLARK: Look. I've been busy. It's a minority government, and, well, you've got eyes, I've had a rough few months.

MULRONEY: Sure. The budget alone . . .

CLARK: It's eating up a lot of time. So while I appreciate—

MULRONEY: Joe, I'm gonna stop you there. The fact is you haven't made any appointments, true?

CLARK: True. But—

MULRONEY: We think you should.

CLARK: Okay. In the new year I'll put a committee together to look at making some appoint—

MULRONEY: No. Now.

CLARK: Now?

MULRONEY: In case, you know . . .

CLARK: In case what?

MULRONEY: *(looking around)* In case the otevay doesn't ogay your ayway.

A beat while CLARK *deciphers this.*

CLARK: You want me to appoint some people right now, in case I lose the budget vote?

MULRONEY: Yeah.

CLARK: And just how many appointments would you like me to make in the few minutes remaining before the vote?

MULRONEY: Ah! Hang on.

MULRONEY *digs in a pocket. He comes up with two typewritten pages, stapled together. He consults the second page.*

A hundred and three. No, wait, that doesn't sound right.

He digs around in the same pocket. Comes up with another page.

This one came off. Uhhh . . . ah! A hundred and EIGHTY-three.

CLARK: You're kidding.

MULRONEY: Our understanding is, get this into the clerk of the Privy Council's hands right now, and they happen. Even if the vote later doesn't, you know, happen for you.

CLARK: I can't do it.

MULRONEY: Sorry?

CLARK: I won't do it.

MULRONEY: Uh, Joe, this needs to happen.

CLARK: This is a minority government. I can't start slinging pork when we have such a tenuous hold on power.

MULRONEY: My understanding is, Joe, that's precisely when you have to do it. Here.

CLARK: No. I won't take your list.

MULRONEY: Here!

CLARK: No! Brian! No!

MULRONEY: Take it!

CLARK: No!

MULRONEY: Take it!

They're struggling awkwardly. MULRONEY *gives up.*

Listen. You—if you lose this fucking thing, and you run in an election, there are a lot of people who aren't going to pick up the phone when you call around looking for help.

CLARK: If I run in an election, I can't do it looking like some slimy opportunist who made a hundred and eighty-three appointments just before losing office.

MULRONEY: You stupid . . . I mean, you're just dumb. I can't believe I—

CLARK: What. You can't believe you what?

MULRONEY: Nothing.

CLARK: You can't believe you lost to me?

MULRONEY: I mean, who are you? You're nobody! I lost to a nobody who can barely speak French and has no standing in Quebec. You know why I lost to you? The only reason? I spent too much money! Can you believe it! I spent too much money, looked too professional, and the Robert Stanfield hicks in the party went: oh, Mulroney's too slick, too smart; he looks too much like he should be the next prime minister; no, forget him, we'd better choose the doofus from out West who looks like he fell off a turnip truck! If turnips were made out of brown fuckin' corduroy!

CLARK: Probably you should go, Brian.

MULRONEY: I mean, if I didn't have such a sweet job now, I probably would have killed myself after losing to you.

Projection:

> *Mulroney entered a significant depression after losing the leadership to Clark. Recovering from it prompted him to quit drinking.*

I'm doing something important now. I'm running a company that actually has an impact on people's lives, and I'm making a difference to people. People need steel. Everyone does.

CLARK: That's great, Brian; I'm happy you landed on your—

MULRONEY: And I'm making four times what you make. More! Like five times.

CLARK: Brian. Brian! I get it. And I'm glad for you. But I've got a thing in a little bit, and it's kind of important, and I wonder if—

MULRONEY: I've done important things too!

CLARK: Yes, I know, I—

John CROSBIE is at the door. He doesn't immediately see MULRONEY. Projection:

John Crosbie.

CROSBIE: Joe! Listen. The bathroom attendant in the parliamentary restaurant, his name is Claude, you know him, well, turns out he's from Corner Brook. If we can get three or four Liberals or NDPs into the bathroom just before the vote, Claude can lock the door and they'll be trapped—

CLARK: John. John!

CROSBIE stops. He sees MULRONEY. In CROSBIE's current state, MULRONEY's presence here is too much to process.

CROSBIE: What's he doing here? WHAT IS HE DOING HERE?

MULRONEY: Hey, John Crosbie . . .

CLARK: He was just—

CROSBIE: What in the holy name of fuck is going on here?

CLARK: Nothing. John! John. Nothing's going on. Brian was just leaving. Will you walk him out?

CROSBIE: Okay, but—

CLARK: Brian, thanks for stopping by. I'll talk to you soon.

MULRONEY: Do the thing I said. The list.

CLARK: I'll think about it.

MULRONEY: Do it, you pile of dirt!

CLARK: Oookay. See you soon. Okay, Brian? Okay, John? Talk to you later, okay?

CROSBIE and MULRONEY are leaving, practically hand in hand.

CROSBIE: So, how's the private sector?

MULRONEY: I make a shit-ton of money. I wouldn't come back to politics if you paid me . . .

They're gone. But CROSBIE returns and sticks his head in the door.

Projection:

John Crosbie.

CROSBIE: *(whisper-shouting)* CLAAAAAAUUUUUDE! FROOM COOOORNER BROOOOOOK!

CLARK: Uh huh. You bet. Okay, John.

CLARK's alone. He goes to the stereo, hits a button. It plays Diana Krall: "Boulevard of Broken Dreams." The music is soft.

Projection:

Oh God, more reading:

*After Clark lost the 1980 election the PCs held a party confer-
ence. Part of the conference was a leadership review, standard
procedure after an election loss.*

*Brian Mulroney paid Clark's point man in Quebec,
Rodrigue Pageau, to spy on Clark.*

*An anti-Clark faction in the PC leadership, angry over his
lack of patronage appointments, bought party memberships for
hundreds of people and flew them to the convention. These
new delegates were paid in cash and instructed to vote against
Clark. Clark's support at the convention came in at 66.9%.*

*Although many thought this was a strong enough endorsement of
his leadership, Clark chose to resign and run against Mulroney
for the leadership of the party.*

*After 4 ballots, Mulroney defeated Clark and became leader of
the party, despite the fact he had never been elected to public
office in his life.*

*At least some of the cash that bought the convention delegates
came from a lobbyist whose client later received an enormous
contract from the Mulroney government.*

CLARK *sits. He puts his face in his hands.*

*A young man appears at the door. He's holding a canvas pouch with the
seal of the United States on it.* CLARK *finally notices him.*

CLARK: Hi.

Nothing from the YOUNG MAN.

Is that . . . ?

Still nothing.

Son. Is that for me?

YOUNG MAN: Yes. Yes, sir. Sorry.

CLARK: Well, c'mere.

He brings the pouch to CLARK. CLARK unzips the bag. The YOUNG MAN is leaving.

Stay. I just want to have a look at this, then you can return it to Minister MacDonald.

YOUNG MAN: Okay. Sorry.

CLARK: No no.

The YOUNG MAN waits. The music continues. CLARK takes out a passport, flips through it.

He stops at a page. Examines something. Closes the passport. He's about to return it to the pouch when he stops. He looks closely at a stamp in the passport.

What the . . .

He takes out another passport, checks a stamp in it. He shoves the passport in the pouch, and stares at the ceiling.

Aw, c'mon.

He shuts off the music.

YOUNG MAN: Sir?

CLARK: In Iran. The calendar they use is . . . ?

YOUNG MAN: Pretty sure they use the Persian calendar in Iran.

CLARK: So am I. I'm pretty sure too. For . . . For fuck's sake!

YOUNG MAN: Sir?

CLARK: These stamps are wrong. They have the wrong dates, dates from *our* calendar on the entry stamps. Not the Persian calendar.

Projection:

> **The CIA forgers made this mistake. All of the faked pass-ports had to be redone.**

YOUNG MAN: What are those, sir?

CLARK: You know, I'm not the smartest guy. I know that. I'm not clever. It's not my thing, and I'm fine with that. Clever is good, there's a use for clever. But when everyone is striving for clever, this is the kind of mistake that can happen. When you get so taken by your clever idea, details like this get overlooked. And then people friggin' die.

The YOUNG MAN, *impassive, waits.*

I'm sorry I cursed.

YOUNG MAN: Not at all, sir.

CLARK: What's your name?

YOUNG MAN: Steve, sir.

Projection:

> *It was 1985 when Stephen Harper started working on Parliament Hill. In 1979 he was actually working in the mail room at Imperial Oil in Edmonton.*

> *But what the hell.*

CLARK: Steve, I don't know if you have any ambition to work in politics. You're young. You should probably get the hell out of Ottawa and make something of your life.

HARPER: You don't believe that, sir.

CLARK: Don't I?

HARPER: No, you don't. You wouldn't be here if you did.

CLARK: Yeah. You're right.

HARPER: People say things they don't believe to young people to assert dominance over them.

CLARK: Is that what I was doing?

HARPER: I think so. You've had a shock. Something in that bag is immensely frustrating to you. I'm standing here, I'm nobody, so you say something cynical and, uh, *worldly* to me to dominate me.

CLARK: You're . . . You're absolutely right.

HARPER: I've been here a while, I'm nobody, people do it to me all the time.

A beat.

You're having a rotten day.

CLARK: Well, the day's not over yet.

HARPER: You're going to lose the vote later?

CLARK: Looks that way.

HARPER: What a waste.

CLARK: I don't disagree, but in what way, exactly, do you mean it's a waste?

HARPER: No, never mind, sir. Not my place.

CLARK: I'm asking. I'd like your opinion, Steve.

HARPER: Okay. Well, let me ask you: does Margaret Thatcher's victory earlier this year not inspire you?

Projection:

    Thatcher came to power in Britain in May 1979 in a landslide.

CLARK: I assume it inspires you?

HARPER: It does. It really does.

CLARK: The magnitude of her win?

HARPER: That's part of it. She ran a campaign that didn't shy away from controversial topics or hard choices, and she won huge.

CLARK: Unlike my campaign, which took a careful middle road and won small.

HARPER is silent.

Canada and Britain are very different places.

HARPER: Sure.

CLARK: She can say harsh things about what she feels is wrong with her country and get away with it. She can alienate half the population, more than half, and still win. That's not the way we do things here.

HARPER: But you don't need a majority of Canadians to vote for your party for you to win, either.

CLARK: But I need to act like I do.

HARPER: Why?

CLARK: It's called responsible government for a reason. If I lead the country, I act in the interests of everyone in the country, whether they vote for me or not.

HARPER: But that's impossible. The country is too big, too fragmented to be acting in everyone's interests at all times.

CLARK: It's complicated, but not impossible. You look at the totality of your choices as Prime Minister, and the goal is to serve the country as a whole through those choices.

HARPER: Which leads, inevitably, to a ballooning bureaucracy, to overspending and more deficits. It's just . . .

CLARK: It's just what?

HARPER: No. I'm sorry, sir. I won't take up any more of your time.

CLARK: No, I'm curious. Stay. This is practically the first grown-up conversation I've had all day. You wish we could have a Thatcherite revolution right here in Canada. What exactly is it about our politics you feel is lacking?

HARPER: Sanity.

CLARK: Uh! Uh! Uh! Agreed. But can you be more specif—

HARPER: Unemployment insurance. A program created to help an individual who suddenly loses their job while they look for a new one? Is now used to prop up a whole region where work is seasonal.

CLARK: The fishery couldn't survive without it. Provincial assistance programs are inadequate. Without UI the economy of the Maritimes collapses.

HARPER: So?

A beat.

CLARK: You're not serious.

HARPER: You're not serious when you make a statement like "the economy of the Maritimes collapses." The fishery changes. Maybe it survives, maybe it doesn't. But if it doesn't, the people in those provinces, they figure it out. Give them credit.

CLARK: The hardship would be enormous. Imagine being the prime minister who allowed that to happen on his watch.

HARPER: I have two points. One: the ocean is getting overfished because there are so many government-subsidized people fishing, which will inevitably lead to the collapse of the fishery anyway; and two: if it can't survive without massive government support, it can't properly be called an economy.

Projection:

The cod fishery collapsed from overfishing in 1992.

And now you're thinking: "But I need the votes that come from Atlantic Canada."

CLARK: Yes, I was.

HARPER: I say you don't, but let that go for now. You're now justifying the perversion, the *abuse* of a perfectly decent social program to save your skin politically.

CLARK: If I write off an entire region of the country with one decision I deserve to lose their votes.

HARPER: I'm telling you consistency is what matters. People need to be told the truth, not be taken care of. That's what I take from Thatcher's victory.

CLARK: She said what she was going to do, and she did it.

HARPER: She said it simply, directly, and without worrying about whose feelings got hurt. She ran on a five-point plan, and she's been pursuing the plan since she was elected. How many bills have you passed since coming to power?

CLARK: Six.

HARPER: Three.

CLARK: No, pretty sure it's six bills.

HARPER: Three were old bills proposed by the previous, *Liberal* government.

CLARK: Things we would have done anyway. Passing bills initiated by the Liberals spoke to the co-operative relationship we hoped to have with the opposition.

HARPER: Yeah! How's that going for you?

A pause. HARPER's gone too far.

Sorry.

CLARK: You know what—

HARPER: I'm sorry. It's a terrible fault of mine. I get worked up, and I become disrespectful, and it's a terrible fault. I apologize.

CLARK: It's okay.

HARPER: No one asks me for my thoughts. I'm out of practise. I'm sorry, sir. I'm sorry.

CLARK: It's not a problem. Steve—

HARPER: No, it is. I have to fix that.

(to himself) Jeez. C'mon.

CLARK: It's okay. Go on with what you were saying.

HARPER: No, sir. I think I've said enough. Thank you, sir.

CLARK: Steve. It's okay, I'm not mad; I was momentarily surprised. Go on. Margaret Thatcher is great because . . . ?

HARPER: Uhh . . .

CLARK: Five-point plan . . .

HARPER: Yes, sir. She had a five-point plan. It's like a contract with voters.

CLARK: It's a gross oversimplification of the job she's asking for.

HARPER: In some ways, yes. But isn't part of her job being able to communicate with the people she's meant to serve? And isn't simplicity central to effective communication?

CLARK: You admire her communications strategy.

HARPER: I admire her unneurotic relationship with the public.

CLARK: Her relationship with the public seems unnecessarily harsh to me.

HARPER: Can I— Can I share with you an observation I've made about politics? And politicians?

CLARK: Can I stop you if I've heard it before?

HARPER: Absolutely. Okay. Say you're a bunny.

CLARK: A bunny?

HARPER: Yes. Say you're a bunny.

CLARK: Okay. I'm a bunny.

HARPER: Fluffy, bottom of the food chain, everybody eats you and you eat nobody.

CLARK: I'm gentle; I'm delicious.

HARPER: Yes. And you live in the woods. In a dell.

CLARK: And I live in a dell.

HARPER: Woodsy hills all around, and your warren is in a clearing.

CLARK: A clearing in the dell.

Projection:

> *A picture, or video, of a leafy forest. A clearing in that forest.*

HARPER: Surrounded by woods, woods, woods, and you're a bunny, and you live with the other bunnies at one end of the clearing. You and the other bunnies in your warren, you get hungry. A lot. And across the dell, other side of the clearing, is a lot of lettuces. Really a lot. But between you and the lettuces is a den full of foxes. You've learned this through experience.

CLARK: Okay.

HARPER: Your dad got killed by the foxes.

CLARK: Okay.

HARPER: Or no, better: your mother got killed. Your mother got torn apart by some foxes.

CLARK: Got it.

HARPER: Your life is exactly two things: eat the lettuces, keep from getting eaten by the foxes.

CLARK: That's my whole deal as a bunny.

HARPER: Those two things. Stuff lettuces, avoid the foxes. Now: going around the dell, deep in the hilly woods to avoid the foxes and getting to the lettuce costs almost as many calories as you gain by stuffing yourself with lettuce. You're just as hungry by the time you return to the warren if you take the long way.

CLARK: And going straight through the dell means risking getting my furry self eaten by a fox. Like Ma.

HARPER: Yes. You see what I'm saying?

A beat.

CLARK: Are you asking me if I understand this analogy as it relates to political behaviour?

HARPER: You don't.

CLARK: Gonna need a little bit more, Steve.

HARPER: Weird. Okay. Take the long way to the lettuce and suffer calorically, or take the direct route to the lettuces and risk death. You have to make some version of that choice every day. And you're always tempted to compromise each of these goals, a little, in favour of the other. You can even convince yourself that there's a balance to be found between them. Maybe I can risk a tiny bit of danger to keep more lettuce calories. But the truth is, you eventually either get eaten or starve. Because the two goals can't be blended. They are unblendable.

CLARK: Okay . . .

HARPER: That's being a politician. There are two things going on: politics and policy. You make decisions all day long, and those decisions are either about politics, acquiring and maintaining power, or policy, doing things that further the country.

CLARK: And I'm tempted continually to blend them?

HARPER: My observation is this: politicians blend politics and policy all day long. And if you're in power, you call everything policy. "All I do is in the service of you, the people that elected me." And that's not true. Some of your time is spent grasping for power, but it's hidden away, it's a secret. And so now you're in a dishonest relationship with the people you lead.

CLARK: I think voters can tell when I'm acting in the public interest and when I'm running for re-election.

HARPER: I'd suggest that YOU can't even tell most of the time. Your response to the idea of ending UI for fishermen is two things at once: "There will be enormous suffering" and "They'll stop voting for me." One is policy, the other is politics. You blend them so you don't have to face the fact that, much of the time, you're just trying to keep your job, not do good. You're not only in a dishonest relationship with voters, you're lying to yourself.

CLARK: I see. And let me guess: you wish I'd do some radical thing, like move my bunny warren to the other side of the dell and avoid the foxes altogether?

HARPER: Well, in my head, you take a garden hose and stick it in the fox den and drown all the foxes, but okay, sure, your thing.

CLARK: You think I need to abandon politics for pure policy.

HARPER: No! I think exactly the opposite.

CLARK: What!

HARPER: You spend entirely too much time trying to do good for people.

CLARK: You're serious!

HARPER: Too much policy. Not enough politics. The thing I admire most about Mrs. Thatcher is that ninety percent of her actions are motivated by politics. She spends all of her time making moves that solidify her base. It's clear, unambiguous politicking. Of the dozens of bills she's managed to pass since May, all but probably two are politically motivated.

CLARK: That's the grossest perversion of what I would consider a leader's job.

HARPER: A leader's job is one thing and one thing only: hegemony.

CLARK: Hegemony?

HARPER: Hegemony.

CLARK: Complete domination of the populace? The accumulation of all available power?

HARPER: More or less, sure.

CLARK: Dictatorship?

HARPER: Dictatorship's not possible in a democracy, and probably not a worthwhile goal from a moral standpoint.

CLARK: Phew! Glad to hear it. Nice to know where the line is.

HARPER: In a democracy, hegemony means convincing the citizenry that your point of view is the objective truth. That the things you believe are actually the way things are.

CLARK: Being persuasive, getting people on side, sure, these are fundamental to success as a politician.

HARPER: I'm not wild about persuasion. The problem with convincing people is that it invites rebuttal. Conversation leads to the consideration of the other side, which leads to consensus building, which leads to weak policy.

CLARK: Otherwise known as democracy.

HARPER: No! Democracy is the entry point. Once elected, democracy ends. You're hired to lead, to pursue your agenda—pursue it!

CLARK: There are a ton of reasons why I can't just ignore everyone and do what I feel like doing, thank God. Power is also distributed among the provinces.

HARPER: They have their powers, you have yours.

CLARK: Doesn't work that way. Quebec alone has enough seats that I have to consider how a particular policy effects—

HARPER: You don't need Quebec.

CLARK: Sorry?

HARPER: You don't need Quebec.

CLARK: I don't need Quebec?

HARPER: You don't need Quebec.

CLARK: Every Canadian prime minister since the dawn of time has had to attract enough support from Quebec to get anything done.

HARPER: You don't need Quebec. But let me say what I—

CLARK: No, wait, hang on—

HARPER: No. Let me finish my point!

A beat. HARPER has once again gone too far.

CLARK: Go ahead, Steve. Make your point.

HARPER: Okay. Well. I'm not talking about a province's power or getting a piece of legislation through or how you engage the opposition. I'm talking about true hegemony: when the fabric of the nation is made by you. When your influence reaches down to the level where people aren't aware of it. When the country chooses a new flag, and the colours of the country's new flag happen to also be your political party's colours. And nobody objects.

Projection:

> *The colours of the flag of Canada, adopted in 1965, are red and white.*

The most exciting thing for me about Mrs. Thatcher's victory is that she's building something so durable she will, over time, change the fabric of her country.

Projection:

> *Once Thatcher was elected the Conservative Party stayed in power for 18 years.*

CLARK: Policies come and go, but hegemony is forever.

HARPER: Exactly. How many of Trudeau's policies were you hoping to walk back? How many things did you want to change that, if you did, would simply get changed back when the Liberals return to power?

CLARK: Meanwhile, the flag of the country stays red and white.

HARPER: Exactly, sir.

Projection:

> *Of the 100 years of the twentieth century the Liberal Party formed the government of Canada for 70.*

CLARK: So from your perspective, my putting all my chips on this budget getting passed is foolish?

HARPER is silent.

From your perspective, is there *ever* a time when a leader should put principles above longevity?

HARPER: Longevity is the principle, sir.

A pause. CLARK *starts to move around the room, opening and shutting wood-panelled doors.*

CLARK: I'm looking for . . . I'm looking for a closet large enough to hold your lifeless corpse, Steve.

HARPER: Sir?

CLARK: I feel like the greatest service I can offer the country at this moment is to make sure your ideas are never disseminated.

HARPER: Oh, that's a joke! Killing me's unnecessary, sir. There's no chance the things I want to see happen will happen. Your government is the closest we were ever gonna get, and it wasn't that close.

CLARK: I'm as close to Thatcher as Canada's going to get?

HARPER: You, personally, have qualities that would have made a Canadian right-wing revolution possible. Setting aside your left-wing beliefs, of course.

CLARK: My left-wing . . . ?

HARPER: So co-opted are you by Liberal hegemony, most of the policies you're struggling to get thought Parliament, which you believe to be centre-right, are in reality centre-left.

CLARK: I believe I have an idea about why you're rarely encouraged to speak, Steve. And what are the qualities I possess that, if it weren't for my utterly co-opted politics, make me the ideal leader of a Canadian conservative revolution?

HARPER: You're from Alberta. Power is shifting west, and there's never been a Western-born prime minister.

CLARK: Diefenbaker! No, he was born in Ontario.

HARPER: Ontario, yes. You're the first one, and that alone unlocks vast amounts of support for you, if only you'd exploit it.

CLARK: Not interested in playing regions against each other.

HARPER: I'm aware. But if you were, you could remain in power for a decade. The other quality you possess is: you're a forgettable blank. A nobody.

CLARK: I'm a nobody.

HARPER: A complete nobody. You're the leader of this country, and the vast majority of Canadians couldn't pick you out of a police lineup.

CLARK: I see.

HARPER: And that's good. Because here's how our revolution would've been different from Thatcher's: we are a people that avoids confrontation. Britons need it; they thrive on it; it's how they built an empire. We hate it. And so, as long as the leader is as still, silent, and blank as possible . . . he can do whatever he wants.

CLARK: But you have to communicate; you have to be visible. You have to *lead*, for God's sake.

HARPER: My guess is that Canadians are sort of over being led. If someone tried leaving them alone, they'd probably be okay with that.

CLARK: But Trudeau! He's the most popular politician the country's ever seen.

HARPER: And you defeated him.

CLARK: And I'm nobody.

HARPER: You are. That's why it's such a waste. The moment is right for a conservative revolution—Britain has hers, America is about to get its own. You're perfectly situated to give us ours, and in a few minutes you're going to throw it all away.

CLARK: If I can't get this budget through, I don't deserve to govern.

HARPER: Let me ask you: do you believe that if you allow what's about to happen to happen, that history will say you're a principled person? That Joe Clark gave up power because his conscience told him to?

CLARK: I've no idea.

HARPER: Let me end the suspense for you: it will not. History will say you were weak-willed and incompetent.

Another beat.

CLARK: Okay.

HARPER: Let me implore you, sir, probably at the expense of my job: think for yourself. Do what needs to be done. Ignore Quebec. For every vote you lose there you'll pick up two west of Brockville. Acknowledge the power the West has and recognize that every time the price of oil rises, that power increases. Think for yourself, and forget Ontario—stop pretending you're a member of the Ontario elite. Ontario is the past, and the West is the future. Believe in people, in their resilience and ability to adapt. The more you ask of people, the more they'll respect you. The more you convince them that relying on the state for anything is wrong, the more they'll respect you. I know that somewhere inside you is a true conservative politician. Find it. Find it, sir.

CLARK: Steve—

HARPER: Sir, who knows if the country will ever have this chance again. Be the person the country needs you to be, sir, Mr. Clark. Not the person you are!

CLARK: Hey!

HARPER: Don't let Trudeau have the country back. He'll just pass it to Mulroney, and God only knows what he'll do to it. I can't bear to think of what will happen if you do this, sir. Don't do this, Mr. Clark. There are half a dozen procedural ways for you to avoid this vote.

CLARK: Steve!

The division bell is ringing, calling MPs to vote. A pause.

HARPER: Sir—

CLARK: Steve, I have to go.

HARPER: But— Yes, sir.

CLARK: Thanks for the chat.

HARPER: It wasn't . . . that wasn't a chat.

HARPER is leaving.

CLARK: Steve: I asked you before. Do you have any interest in pursuing politics as a career?

HARPER: Oh, no, sir. I'm going to go back to university and get a degree in economics.

CLARK: Really? Economics?

HARPER: I find it's, um, more nuanced than politics. Politics is a blunt instrument. It's clumsy. Irrational. It's . . .

CLARK: Shabby. I agree.

HARPER: Yes. I was going to say: inelegant.

CLARK: Yes. Inelegant. A better word. But you're passionate, and that would take you a long way in this business.

HARPER: I consider passion a huge liability for a politician, sir.

CLARK: I was . . . I was trying to pay you a compliment, Steve.

HARPER: I know you were, sir.

A pause as the two regard each other. Suddenly, HARPER goes to CLARK. He shakes CLARK's hand.

Thank you, sir. Thank you very much for talking to me.

HARPER goes. CLARK sits. After a long beat he hits the remote. "Que Sera, Sera," the live version by Corinne Bailey Rae, plays.

Flora MACDONALD arrives at the door. Projection:

Flora MacDonald.

MACDONALD: You coming?

CLARK: Yes. Let's get it over with.

He rises.

Oh, by the way, don't let me forget, there's a problem with those stupid fake passports that would probably result in the deaths of all involved if they get used.

MACDONALD: Oh dear.

CLARK: Let's try to keep that in mind. We're going to be busy later.

MACDONALD: Okay.

CLARK: I'll see you down there.

She's leaving.

Flora? Thanks.

MACDONALD: Thank you, Joe.

She goes.

After a few moments, CLARK *takes off his brown jacket. He rubs his face with it.*

These projections run during the following action:

> **The Progressive Conservatives lost the confidence vote 139–133.**

CLARK *balls up the coat, shoves it in a closet or drawer.*

*Trudeau led the country during the Quebec referendum of 1980.
His charisma, intelligence, and strength made the difference.
The No side won with 59.6% of the vote.*

*Trudeau's creation of a Charter of Rights and Freedoms,
proposed as part of constitutional reform initiated during the
referendum, transformed the country.*

CLARK *then kicks off his shoes. He hides them under the rug.*

*These are Trudeau's greatest achievements, neither of which
would have occurred had he retired.*

CLARK *sits on the floor, peels off his socks. He stuffs each one into a water
glass.*

*Maureen McTeer wrote the bar exams through the election
of 1980. She passed, and was called to the Ontario bar in
April, 1980.*

*Clark remained a member of Parliament and became Brian
Mulroney's Secretary of State for External Affairs in 1984.*

*Mulroney's decision, in 1986, to award a jet maintenance
contract to a Montreal firm instead of one from the West is
widely seen as the moment that birthed the Reform Party.
It's also the moment that made Stephen Harper renounce the
Progressive Conservative party forever.*

*In 1993, Harper defeated Progressive Conservative Jim
Hawkes to become the Reform MP for Calgary West. It was
Hawkes who, in 1985, gave a young Harper his first job on
Parliament Hill, as an assistant.*

CLARK *removes his vest, hides it somewhere.*

Clark once again became leader of the PCs in 1998. He resisted all attempts to merge his party with Reform.

The Progressive Conservative Party merged with the Reform Party in 2003, soon after Clark stepped down as leader.

He removes his pants, hides them somewhere. Hides his tie.

Until his retirement, and in spite of the fact that the PC party no longer existed, Clark considered himself a Progressive Conservative member of Parliament. He retired in 2004.

CLARK *leaves as the music continues.*

In 2004, Stephen Harper became leader of the Conservative Party of Canada, merging the parties of the right.

HARPER, *now in a contemporary suit, enters and stands behind the desk.*

He won power in 2006, running on a five-point plan. With Harper as leader, the Conservatives won elections in 2006, 2008, and 2011.

Jenni BYRNE, *his senior advisor, enters and stands across the desk. The music snaps off.*

HARPER: So what?

BYRNE: SO WHAT??!

HARPER: Jenni. Why are you so upset?

BYRNE: Why am I—!

HARPER: I admit it's inelegant.

BYRNE: We just passed legislation that fixes the date of the election, so it happens every four years.

HARPER: Correct.

BYRNE: And you propose we ignore that new law, and have an election this October.

HARPER: Correct.

BYRNE: Instead of October of next year. As per our new law.

HARPER: Yup.

BYRNE: Don't you think . . .

HARPER: What? That we'll make people *mad*?

BYRNE: No. Yes! We'll get flayed in the press, the House, everywhere, for ignoring the legislation we just passed.

HARPER: To which I repeat: so what?

BYRNE: The base will hate it too!

HARPER: Oh, the base. The base will be fine. Have you seen this?

He hands her paper.

BYRNE: What's this?

HARPER: Latest polling.

She reads. A pause.

BYRNE: This is . . . This is majority territory.

HARPER: Uh huh.

BYRNE: We're finally polling in majority territory.

HARPER: Uh huh.

BYRNE: Okay. Probably we should have an election this fall instead of waiting until next year.

HARPER: I concur.

BYRNE: And look! We're likely going to pick up seats in Quebec!

HARPER: Yes.

BYRNE: Quebec!

HARPER: Yes.

BYRNE: Get excited, Stephen!

HARPER: I am excited, Jenni. This is me excited.

Projection:

The Right Honourable Joe Clark.

CLARK appears at the door.

CLARK: Excuse me. Hi.

HARPER looks up. BYRNE turns.

Hi. I was just in the building. Thought I'd say hi.

HARPER: Hello.

Projection:

May 27, 2008.

CLARK: They're putting up my portrait. Finally. Are you . . . ?

HARPER: Am I . . . ?

CLARK: Planning to attend. It's in ten minutes.

BYRNE *exits, squeezing past* CLARK.

BYRNE: Excuse me. Congratulations, sir.

CLARK: Ms. Byrne. *(looking around)* Boy, I don't miss this place.

HARPER: No, I expect you don't.

CLARK, *relaxed and cheerful, wanders into the room.* HARPER *watches him.*

CLARK: Boy. I never really noticed at the time, but this office is just . . . It's wood, wood, wood. Isn't it?

CLARK *wanders. He opens a cabinet. It's empty.*

I used to have a big old sound system in here. Very elaborate.

HARPER: I don't listen to a lot of music.

CLARK: Oh? I thought you were a big Beatles guy.

HARPER *waits. Music begins: "It's Hard to Be a Saint in the City" by Bruce Springsteen. The live version from the Hammersmith Odeon concert in 1975.*

Anyway. Sorry! You coming?

The two men look at each other.

Projection:

> **Harper did not attend the ceremony.**

The music swells. Projection:

> **In 2015, the Liberals returned, once again, to power.**

Blackout.

THE END

ACKNOWLEDGEMENTS

The play is, of course, a work of fiction.

I'm grateful to Jeffrey Simpson and John Ibbitson, both of whom provided insight into the events the play covers.

My thanks to Moira and Alison Lawrence for their input.

Jackie Maxwell originally commissioned the play for the Shaw Festival, and I'll always be grateful to her for that. Development input came from Miles Potter, Laurel Green, Tim Carroll, Eric Coates, and Morwyn Brebner. Workshop readings were sponsored by the Shaw Festival and Alberta Theatre Projects.

My thanks to Pam Winter for her relentless, now decades-long support.

Michael Healey is one of Canada's leading theatrical voices. Some of his plays include *Courageous*, *The Drawer Boy*, *Proud*, and *Rune Arlidge*, among others. With an outstanding breadth of work, Michael has won a number of awards as a playwright, including Dora Mavor Moore awards, a Governor General's Literary Award for Drama, and a Chalmers Canadian Play Award. He lives in Toronto.

First edition: April 2017
Printed and bound in Canada by Imprimerie Gauvin, Gatineau

Author photo © John Healey
Cover art by Friction Creative

PLAYWRIGHTS
CANADA PRESS

202-269 Richmond St. W.
Toronto, ON
M5V 1X1

416.703.0013
info@playwrightscanada.com
www.playwrightscanada.com
@playcanpress

MIX
Paper from
responsible sources
FSC
www.fsc.org   FSC® C100212